DOMINIE READERS

Timothy Turtle

Story by Janie Spaht Gill, Ph.D.
Illustrations by Bob Reese

DOMINIE PRESS
Pearson Learning Group

2

Timothy thought,
"I'm out of school,
and I'd like to visit Mike."

"I'm not sure how I'll travel.
I could ride on my bike.

But my tire has a flat,
and I haven't got a pump."

"I could roll on my roller skates, but the road is full of bumps."

"I could skate on my skateboard,

but the weather's very hot."

"I could fly in an airplane, but that would cost a lot."

11

12

"I could ride in a bus,
but it makes lots of stops."

"I could drive in my jeep,

but it hasn't got a top."

"I could ride on a train,

but it makes a lot of sound."

"I could ride in my motorboat,

but the lake is out of town."

"Oh, dear," he thought
as he looked across the floor.

"I guess I'll walk, because,
after all, my friend lives
just next door."

■ Have the children play a transportation game in which one child acts out a mode of transportation and the other children guess what he or she is doing.

■ Ask the children to name the modes of transportation featured in the book. As they name each form of transportation, write it on a chart. Arrange the modes of transportation according to speed, from the fastest to the slowest. They could also be arranged in alphabetical order. You can extend this activity by naming additional modes of transportation that are not depicted in the book.

■ Have the children paint a mural of a small town, with roads, hills, houses, a river, and a bridge. They can draw the buildings on construction paper, cut them out, and paste them onto the mural. Then they can draw various modes of transportation and glue them onto the mural in the appropriate places.

About the Author

Dr. Janie Spaht Gill brings twenty-five years of teaching experience to her books for young children. During her career thus far, she has taught at every grade level, from kindergarten through college. Gill has a Ph.D. in reading education, with a minor in creative writing. She is currently residing in Lafayette, Louisiana with her husband, Richard. Her fresh, humorous topics are inspired by the things her students say in the classroom. Gill was voted the 1999-2000 Louisiana Elementary Teacher of the Year for her outstanding work in primary education.

Softcover Edition ISBN 0-7685-2156-4
Library Bound Edition ISBN 0-7685-2464-4

Printed in Singapore
      5 6 7 8 9 10   10 09 08 07

**Dominie
Press**

Pearson Learning Group

**1-800-321-3106
www.pearsonlearning.com**